Present To:

_____

From:

_____

Date:

_____

30 Days of Hope
Change your energy. Change your life.
© 2022 by Dana M. Bell

ISBN978-1-387-85462-2 (Paper Back)
Imprint/Publisher: Lulu.com

Copyright License. All Rights Reserved - Standard Copyright. No portion of this book may be reproduced, stored in a retrieval system, or transmitted in any form or by any means - electronic , mechanical, photocopy, recording, scanning, or other - except for brief quotations in critical reviews or articles, without the prior written permission of the author, Dana M. Bell.

Contributors:

Help at its best: Vivid Visual Solutions, Lisa Noble, Marketing & Branding; Aspiring Writers Association of America (AWAOA), Cynthia L. Hatcher, Founder; Cynthia M. Pritchett, (poems)

30 Days of Hope
Change Your Energy. Change Your Life.

Dana M. Bell, MA, LLPC

Dedication

This devotional is dedicated to all that need some self-encouragement. There will be times when you will need to be your own best cheerleader. There will also be times where you have to evaluate your negative self-talk and take action to silence it. It's my desire that this book will help you to become stronger in mind, body, and soul.

Thanks

Thanks be to God for all of His Love, Grace, and Mercy!
Thanks to all the beautiful souls from my Past, in my Present and that will be in my Future.

30 Days of Hope

THE PAST IS THE PAST
MY FUTURE IS AMAZING
AND IT STARTS RIGHT NOW

~ C. M. Pritchett

Day 1

SMILE

Smiles lighten your heart and brighten a room. The energy behind a smile has the power to invite more smiles and great experiences. They are free to give and priceless in spirit.

Scientific studies have shown that smiling releases endorphins, natural painkillers, and serotonin. Smiling is natural medicine.

Action Step: Smile!

30 Days of Hope

Day 2

Don't Welcome Misery

When someone approaches you with negativity, gossip and plain ole ugliness, you don't have to be nice and listen to it. Why welcome negative spirits? Stay focused on the Good of Life and pleasant vibrations.

"Create in me a clean heart, O God; and Renew a right spirit within me." *Psalm 51:10 (KJV)*

Action Step: Ask the Creator to help you guard your heart and mind against negativity and to focus on the promises that are laid out for you.

Day 3

Be Grateful

Stay grateful! It's easy to overlook, forget or disregard God's promised blessings we receive every day. Slow your pace today and give thanks to the Almighty forces that bring your health, wealth, joy, and life.

Action Step: Show gratitude for three things. If you smile, give thanks for 3 more. Maybe you are happy with the taste of jellybeans or a morning run. Maybe the thought of the holidays brings you joy. Think about these things to keep you in alignment with your goals, peace, joy and give thanks.

Enjoy your blessed day!

30 Days of Hope

Day 4

Do You!

Do you. People often use this phrase to say something witty or to tell a person to mind their business and worry about themselves. But if you stop and think about it, you will see its true meaning. Do you!

In order to do you, one must Scio te Ipsum Latin for, "know thyself." Genuinely, seek out to know thyself. Learn and pay attention to your feelings and thoughts. Embrace the understanding of the good and not so good about yourself. Try each day to do things that you like. No matter how small the effort, do you!

Action Step: Do what makes you happy and brings you joy. Do what makes your insides smile. Do what makes your brain relax and your body sigh.

Day 5

Positive Thinking

I CAN!

I WILL!

I AM!

I can build a better life for myself!
I will accomplish my goals!
I am strong, magnificent, and in harmony!

"For as he thinketh in his heart, so is he," *Proverbs 23:7 (KJV)*

Action Step: See yourself walking, running, working, and living in the places and spaces where you want to be. Sit and think about the steps you will need to take, and the energy you need to create to become successful.

30 Days of Hope

Day 6

Accept Peace

After dealing with the wickedness of the world, be it a part of your life or not, it may be hard to accept Peace when it comes. Sometimes peace can come when someone lets you cut in front of them in the grocery store line, but you decline. Other times peace can come when out of the blue a friend asks you out to dinner after you have had a rough day.

Peace enters your spirit softly like a breeze. Instead of taking the free, easy moment, you decide to stay in your frustrations and go home. Resistance blocks peace like a brick wall. However, when peace is accepted, it is another blessing to be thankful for.

Action Step: Say yes to Peace. Look for Peace throughout the day. Notice the gentleness of its presence. Stay in that space for as long as you can.

Day 7

Desire More

There's nothing wrong with wanting more.

More strength and wealth

More opportunities and laughter

More peace and joy

More wonderful relationships

Nothing wrong with wanting more. For the more you have, the more you have to give to help others.

Action Step: Ask yourself, "Are my thoughts and actions in alignment with my desires?" If the answer is yes, keep moving and smile. If the answer is no, smile and say to yourself, "I know how to change that." Then, take the necessary action steps you know will match your thoughts and that brilliant smile.

30 Days of Hope

Day 8

Share

You get more when you give more – Universal Law

In case you didn't know, some of your blessings are meant for you to share with others, not keep to yourself. We all have gifts that we were blessed with to help ourselves and others. Some of us sing. Some of us are extremely good in science, which has helped to create advancements in our quality of life. Share yourself.

Action Step: Share in three different ways today. Share your time, talent or treasure in some form or fashion.

Day 9

Welcome Forgiveness

Forgiveness is not for the person that has hurt or upset you.

Forgiveness is not letting someone off the hook for any type of behavior.

Forgiveness is for you!

True forgiveness releases you from pain, heartaches, stress, and strife. It opens the doors of peace, mercy, and joy.

Action Step: Repeat this statement throughout the day: I am at peace. I forgive those that caused pain or confusion in my life. I forgive myself for staying in an unproductive space that caused harmful disruption to my life. I accept my responsibility to make myself happy. I release myself from hurt as I move towards restoration.

Day 10

Feelings Can Be Faulty

Sometimes, we have to push our way through to get over the next hurdle of life. Say a little prayer, take a deep breath, focus your intention on shining through the situation, and go. You'll be blessed! Just because you don't feel like doing something doesn't mean you shouldn't be doing it.

Great motivational speakers will say you must take action to accomplish your goals and obtain your desires. They come to fruition through thought, word, and deed. This means once you have the idea (thought), you write it down or speak it (word) into action (deed).

Action Step: Walk in the direction you want to go in your life! Do one thing every day to reach your goal.

DAY 11

It's Okay to Ask and Accept Help

God's command for us is to love and care for each other. Who are you to deny another person's chance to be blessed through you? As much as you may try, you cannot control everything. There is no shame in having someone help you. Exhale, and allow God's work to be done. He works through others for our good.

Action Step: Graciously accept the love and care from others.

Day 12

Thoughts Become Things

If you think about negative, fearful, and stressful things, those types of experiences will fill your life. Change your experiences by thinking, trusting, and believing in all that is good for your life. Think of all the times you had a plan to accomplish a goal and you were successful. Recall the good feelings you had when you worked through the challenges, and when you achieved your accomplishments. Think of the energy that filled your body as you paved through any negative aspects of your journey. Keep in mind, be it positive or negative, your thoughts, feelings, and energy control the outcome. Since thoughts create things, we need to concentrate on good thoughts and walk in the good feelings.

Action Step: Spend today searching for practical ways to accomplish your goals and smile while you learn.

DAY 13

Don't Worry 'Bout A Thang

Worrying doesn't make anything better. It doesn't fix your problems, and it disrupts your health. I once read somewhere that worrying is like praying for bad things to happen. Cleanse your mind of worry. One of my favorite scriptures is Psalm 37:1-9. This passage always brings me comfort and security. God has got my back. So, smile and give thanks. You don't have to be in control of everything or be perfect.

Action Step: Delight yourself in the Lord. Study His Word. Give Him Praise. Rest in His arms. Stop trying to control situations and outcomes that you have no control over.

Day 14

It's Up to You

If you decide something is going to fail, it will. If you believe something is no good, it isn't. So, if you decide something will be prosperous for your well-being, it will. Don't seek outside forces to assure you of your greatness. Believe in yourself. Trust yourself. We are all made of the superior forces of the Universe. Each of us has the energy made of planets within us. How can you not be great?

> "All our dreams can come true—if we have the courage to pursue them." ~Walt Disney

As Les Brown always says, "There is greatness within you."

Action Step: Accomplish one task today that will help you stay focused on your goal for the week.

DAY 15

What Do You Believe?

Do you believe God has not given us the spirit of fear? Do you believe He has given us the Spirit of a sound mind, joy, peace, and true love for the accepting? If your answer is yes, then why do you live your life in fear-----fear of lack, loss, illness, and poverty. Live and seek what is true!

"Trust in the Lord with all thine heart; and lean not unto thine own understanding. In all your ways submit to him and he will make your paths straight." *Proverbs 3:5-6 (NIV)*

Action Step: Be true to you. Take today and do some self-evaluating and see where it leads you. Ask yourself hard questions and respond accordingly to help yourself reach your highest potential.

Day 16

This Too Shall Pass

All of us will have to walk through some type of event that we deem devastating. We should remember it is a temporary situation. Sometimes it is through no fault of our own. And then, there are those situations where you run full steam ahead into messiness. Each category has some type of lesson for us to learn. The lesson learned comes by how we handle the situation. Some situations will be most trying and hard on the heart. But trust and believe all bring a greater reward.

Action Step: Find a self-development program. Begin growth by understanding yourself. This is a strong way to increase your self-care.

DAY 17

Don't Worry About The "How" of Matters

There are times we don't move forward in our dreams because we can't see how they will manifest. You don't need to know how every step will unfold before you make a move. Just keep taking steps no matter how small towards your goals. God supplies every how as needed. But you must be prepared, motivated, and accepting of the "how's" as they present themselves.

Action Step: Don't overthink the process. Make your move! Do well!

30 Days of Hope

Day 18

Affirmations

Definition: The action or process of affirming something or being affirmed. Positive affirmations can be a very strong tool to combat negativity, decrease anxiety, fears, and worries. When repeated on a regular basis, affirmations will assist with positive thinking.

Action Step: Create fun positive affirmations. Focus on the feeling of having or doing what you say you want. Don't dissect its' truth. Move in the space of it being true. *You create your reality.*

DAY 19

Pay Yourself First

"A part of all you earn is yours to keep."
From the book
The Richest Man in Babylon

Action Step: Start a savings account and put 10% of your earnings into this account. Don't spend from this account. If your mind won't let you put 10% away, then put away what your mind will be comfortable with. Make increases each quarter.

Day 20

Guard Your Heart and Mind

There will always be forces that will attempt to keep you from reaching your goals. These forces wish to cause discord in your family, your job, your heart, and mind. Recognize these forces as they come into your life. Do not allow them to stay and fester. God is not the author of fear or confusion. Therefore, you always have ammunition to expel them from your life.

Action Step: Create fun positive affirmations. Focus on the feeling of having or doing. Be mindful of the company you keep. Discard the takers and users in your life. Be most mindful that you are not the negative force in your life.

DAY 21

Praise Does the Heart Well

Whenever you feel sad or discontent, start giving praise to God. Giving God thanks for all the many true and beautiful things He has done in your life will lift you up. Soon your heart will become light.

Action Step: Say thank you all throughout the day. "Praise the Lord, all ye nations: praise Him, all ye people." *Psalm 117 (KJV)*

"This is the day which the Lord hath made; we will rejoice and be glad in it." *Psalm 118:24 (KJV)*

Day 22

Fear is *not* Stronger than Faith

Eleanor Roosevelt once said, "You gain strength, courage, and confidence by every experience in which you really stop to look fear in the face. You can say to yourself; I have lived through this horror. I can take the next thing that comes along."

Oftentimes, we doubt our ability to prevail over a situation because we are viewing it from the hurt of the moment. We fail to understand that we are created to conquer all that come before us.

Action Step: Encourage yourself with God's word and the positivity of others. Read and reflect on one scripture every day.

DAY 23

Love Yourself First

You must give yourself the respect, honor, and love you deserve first before you can expect it from others.

"If I am not good to myself, how can I expect anyone else to be good to me?"

~ Maya Angelou

Action Step: Love on yourself!

30 Days of Hope

Day 24

Open Your Mind

"Imagination is everything. It is the preview of Life's coming attractions." -Albert Einstein

Self-development is key to living the life you have always dreamed about and God has purposed for you.

Action Step: Read the following books-
10 Pages a day does the mind good.

*The Secrets to Success by Eric Thomas
*The Strangest Secret by Earl Nightingale
*The Power of NOW by Eckhart Tolle
*The Science of Getting Rich by Wallace D. Wattles
*Feeling is the Secret by Neville Goddard
*The Game of Life by Florence Scovel Shinn
*You Can Heal Your Life by Louise Hay
*Ask! By Mark Victor Hansen and Crystal Dwyer Hansen
*Higher Is Waiting by Tyler Perry
*Your Invisible Power by Genevieve Behrend

DAY 25

Self-Development=Self-Care

Self-development is a key component to one's self-care. Understanding your values regarding money, relationships, emotional and mental triggers, along with your likes and dislikes will help you to make stronger and better decisions for your life.

Action Step: Move towards your greatness!
Read the following books:

*Unleash Your Purpose by Dr. Myles Munroe
*The Miracle of Right Thought by Orison Swett Marden
*The Secret of Imagining by Neville Goddard
*I Wish I knew This 20 Years Ago by Justin Perry
*Activate Your Vision by Lucinda Cross
*Wisdom is my Sister and Understanding is my Intimate Friend by Dr. Monique Tucker
*Sacred Pampering Principles by Debrena Jackson-Gandy
*The Instant Millionaire by Mark Fisher
*Exponential Living by Sheri Riley
*The Miracle Morning by Hal Elrod

30 Days of Hope

Day 26

Be Intentional!

Energy Flows Where Attention Goes—

Whether positive or negative your energy will flow where you direct it. So, steer your attention to the positive aspects you want to see come to fruition in your life.

Action Step: Intentionally plan out your day, every day!

DAY 27

Watch Your Speech

Never admit the possibility of failure or speak in a way that makes failure a possibility. Stop giving life to the negative things around you through your speech.

Action Step: Practice looking for the positive in all your situations and seek out the best solution. Not the most comfortable or easiest, but the best.

Day 28

Seek Wisdom

Converse with and read about those persons that have traveled down the roads of success you wish to walk upon. Don't allow naysayers to have a position in your plan.

Action Step: Let this be a motto you can gain strength from, "Whatever the mind of man can conceive it can achieve."

Now create a motto specifically for you.

DAY 29

Don't Block Your Blessings

A hard heart cannot receive true love, joy, or peace. Forgive and set yourself free. Show gratitude to fill your heart with joy. Let blessings flow to you so that you in turn can be a blessing.

Action Step: Think about what past or present hurts you need to release. Then do so. Then allow the blessings of peace to enter your life from all directions. (Some people may need professional assistance to process past hurts or trauma……seek it. Therapy is a great tool!)

30 Days of Hope

Day 30

Self-Assess and Self-Reflect

Every problem has its own seeds of the solution. The solution is usually the opposite of the problem.

Everything you seek is seeking you. Be available in mind, spirit, and body to opportunities.

Never beg anyone to love you. Ever! Would you beg someone to take your gold?

There is greatness in you! You should always walk in that space.

For a better tomorrow you must take action today. Therefore, what we do today sets up our tomorrows.

Believe in yourself.

Be mindful of your emotions when making decisions. Self-assess! Your emotions don't always lead you to the best places. Take a moment to check and see if you are making decisions based on facts, hurt, embarrassment, or jealousy?

If you have not begun to live or recognize your authentic self, start now! Enjoy the journey of learning about you.

SHE WAS SAD AND SCARED
HAD TO MAKE MOVES TO SUCCEED
HER STRENGTH WAS THE KEY

~ C. M. Pritchett

Connect with Dana M. Bell for speaking engagements, digital products, and other books

Instagram and Facebook:
@talkwithdanabell

Email:
talkwithdanabell@gmail.com